This Book Belongs to

For Milt
Taster, critic, peeler, dishwasher, inspiration

The mission of Storey Communications is to serve our customers
by publishing practical information that encourages personal independence
in harmony with the environment.

Edited by Pamela Lappies
Cover and interior illustrations by Mary Rich
Cover and text design by Meredith Maker
Text production by Susan Bernier
Indexed by Northwind Editorial Services

Some recipes have been adapted from other Storey/ Garden Way Publishing books: pages 14, 34: A-106 *Recipes for Gourmet Vegetables* by Glenn Andrews; pages 26, 48, 54: A-40: *Mushroom Cookery* by Jo Mueller; page 35: *Herbal Vinegar* by Maggie Oster; page 44: *The Carrot Cookbook* by Audra and Jack Hendrickson. Recipes on the following pages are used with permission of Delftree Farm, North Adams, Massachusetts (800-243-3742): pages 17, 24, 30, 36.

The information in this book is true and complete to the best of our knowledge. All recommendations are made without guarantee on the part of the author or Storey Communications, Inc. The author

and publisher disclaim any liability in connection with the use of this information. For additional information please contact Storey Communications, Inc., Schoolhouse Road, Pownal, Vermont 05261.

Printed in Canada by Métropole Litho

10 9 8 7 6 5 4 3 2 1

Library of Congress
Cataloging-in-Publication Data

Bass, Ruth, 1934–
   Mushrooms love herbs / Ruth Bass;
      illustrations by Mary Rich.
      p.   cm.
   "A fresh from the garden cookbook."
   ISBN 0-88266-933-8 (hc)
   1. Cookery (Mushrooms) 2. Cookery (Herbs) I. Title.
TX804.B343   1996
641.6′58—dc20   96-14312
                                        CIP

'99 2-

Merry Xmas Bot.
We'll be anxious to taste
your creations.

Larry. Deb

MUSHROOMS LOVE HERBS

A
Fresh from the Garden
Cookbook

RUTH BASS

ILLUSTRATED BY MARY RICH

STOREY

A Storey Publishing Book
Storey Communications, Inc.

Introduction

Mushrooms have a magical quality. Leprechauns lean against them to take a nap, fairies take refuge under their roofs during rainstorms, their very shapes and colors intrigue and delight any woods walker. But like most kinds of magic, mushrooms are not to be trifled with.

A few years ago at an outdoor market in a small Hungarian city, my husband and I marveled at the mushrooms spread out on tables tended by peasant women. The fungi were tawny orange, chocolate brown, eerie green, yellow, white— all sorts of shapes and sizes. Our guide pointed to the mushroom inspector's post, where a woman was deftly sorting through every bag of mushrooms brought to her — by those wishing to sell or by private citizens seeking reassurance. We watched her sweep several mushrooms into a trash container, then put the rest back in a bag and return them to a man in a suit and tie. Many Hungarians, we learned, hunt for wild mushrooms, eat the wrong ones, and are poisoned by them.

Unless you have a mycologist at hand, the market is the safest place to get mushrooms. There the traditional white or button mushrooms are now joined by many varieties of wild mushrooms grown on mushroom farms, all perfectly safe. At Delftree Farm in North Adams, Massachusetts, for instance, the famous Japanese shiitakes are grown in a nineteenth-century textile mill. Delftree shiitakes, which they ship all over the United States, have creamy white gills under a plump, golden-brown cap as large as five inches across. They are high quality and safe. So, the message is: Photograph mushrooms in the woods and eat the ones from the market. Combine them with fresh parsley, oregano, savory, or basil from your vegetable, container, or window-sill garden — and discover double magic.

Another controversy about mushrooms has to do with preparation: Do you wash them or clean them with a brush? Cleaniks can't face cooking a mushroom that hasn't been washed, so they get them all wet and then have to towel them off. Purists say you never wash a mushroom; you just brush it with a mushroom brush. Sometimes we wash, sometimes we brush; if they're going to be served raw, it's best to brush, no matter how you feel about dirt. One compromise is to wipe with a dampened paper towel.

Storage is another question. If you put them in an airtight plastic bag and refrigerate them, you'll end up with a soggy mess in a very short time. Loosely covered, with a piece of paper toweling stuffed into the container, mushrooms keep pretty well in the refrigerator, right next to the fresh basil, sage, savory, and other herbs also available now in most supermarkets.

Buying and storing fresh herbs is less tricky. Look for bright greens, perky leaves, and no moisture in the packaging. You can keep them in their plastic containers or plastic bags, but don't wash them until you're ready to use them. Before chopping, squeeze them in a paper towel — a wet herb is hard to mince.

Once out of the refrigerator and into the pan, mushrooms and herbs blend to create rich and delicate flavors that sometimes will surprise but always will delight.

Porcini Quiche with Parsley and Sage

If you can't find fresh porcini mushrooms, settle for dried and soak them back to life. They'll have most of the rich flavor of their fresh counterparts. Then try them in a quiche that tastes of fresh sage.

2 tablespoons butter
½ pound porcini mushrooms,
    cleaned and chopped
Unbaked 9-inch pie shell (pastry
    recipe, page 44)
6 ounces Swiss cheese, shredded
    (1½ cups)

3 eggs
1 cup light cream
½ cup low-fat milk
1 tablespoon minced fresh sage
1 tablespoon minced fresh parsley
Salt and freshly ground black pepper
¼ teaspoon dry mustard

1. In a medium skillet, melt the butter and sauté the mushrooms over low heat until they are golden but not browned.
2. Cover the bottom of the pie shell with the shredded cheese and the mushrooms. Preheat the oven to 375°F.

3. With an electric mixer, beat the eggs, cream, milk, sage, parsley, salt and pepper to taste, and dry mustard. Pour into the pie shell.

4. Bake for 40 minutes, until firm and browned. Cut into wedges and serve warm.

6 SERVINGS

Herbed Eggs with Crimini

Those who can't eat eggs may live by that edict, but they find it a bore sometimes. Here's a way to give them a breakfast treat using a combination of the yolkless commercial egg product, plus an egg white. If you quadruple the recipe for four, triple the parsley and oregano.

> ½ teaspoon butter
> 2 crimini mushrooms, cleaned and chopped
> 1 teaspoon minced fresh parsley
> 1 teaspoon minced fresh oregano
> ½ garlic clove, minced
> 1 carton yolkless egg product
> 1 egg white

1. In a small skillet, melt the butter, swirling it to coat the bottom and sides of the pan.
2. Add the mushrooms, parsley, oregano, and garlic, and cook over low heat for about 2 minutes, stirring to keep the mixture from getting crisp.
3. In the meantime, whisk the egg product and the egg white together in a small bowl. When the mushrooms are soft and golden, pour in the egg mixture and scramble rapidly.

1 SERVING

Mushroom Salsa with Cilantro

Salsa is everywhere. Sometimes it's fiery hot, sometimes it's mild, and it nearly always includes tomatoes. For a new taste sensation, try it with mushrooms, parsley, and cilantro.

1 large (4- to 5-inch diameter) portabella mushroom
2 ripe tomatoes
4 sprigs parsley, finely chopped
1 tablespoon minced fresh cilantro
Juice of 1 lime
Juice of ½ lemon
1 small onion, minced
1 jalapeño pepper, cored, seeded, and minced

1. Remove the stem from the mushroom, then clean and chop the cap.
2. Dice the tomatoes and combine in a medium-sized bowl with the mushroom. Stir in the parsley, cilantro, lime and lemon juices, onion, and jalapeño pepper.
3. Let stand at room temperature for at least an hour so that the flavors will blend. Stir well and serve with tortilla chips.

ABOUT 2 CUPS

Garlicky Mushroom Spread

For a quick appetizer — something different from raw vegetables and dip — make this mushroom mix ahead of time. Several hours of chilling will allow the flavors of the rosemary and shiitakes to blend. Just take it out of the refrigerator a half hour before serving.

1 bulb garlic
2–3 tablespoons extra virgin olive oil
4 large shallots, finely chopped
½ cup chicken broth
1 pound shiitakes, wiped clean,
    stems discarded

1 teaspoon minced fresh rosemary
2 teaspoons minced fresh Italian
    flat-leaf parsley
1 tablespoon Marsala wine
6 black olives, pitted
Salt and freshly ground black pepper

1. Slice a thin layer off the top of the whole garlic. Brush a little oil in a small ovenproof pan, add the unpeeled garlic head, and drizzle a tablespoon of oil over the top. Roast in a 350°F oven for 15 minutes.
2. In a large skillet, heat the rest of the oil and cook the shallots over low heat, stirring frequently, for about 10 to 12 minutes, or until they are soft. Add the chicken broth, increase the heat, and cook another minute. With a slotted spoon, transfer the shallots to a food processor or blender, leaving all the liquid in the pan.
3. Add the mushrooms to the skillet and cook over medium heat, stirring often. Add the rosemary and parsley and continue cooking until the mushrooms are tender.
4. Pop the roasted garlic cloves out of their skins, and add the mushrooms, garlic, wine, and olives to the processor or blender. Process until creamy. Season with salt and pepper to taste and chill. Serve on plain crackers or rye rounds.

1½ CUPS

Marinated Mushrooms with Thyme

As an appetizer, a salad, or a condiment, these mushrooms are pretty, full of flavor, and close to irresistible. While thyme is often the herb of choice with mushrooms, basil or oregano or sage can be substituted for a change of taste.

4 cups water
½ teaspoon salt
1 pound white button mushrooms
½ cup white wine vinegar
3 shallots, minced
2 teaspoons minced fresh thyme, with tough stems removed
⅛ teaspoon cayenne

1 garlic clove, minced
¼ cup extra virgin olive oil
1 small jar marinated artichoke hearts, undrained, chopped
2 tablespoons finely chopped fresh parsley
Freshly ground black pepper

1. In a large saucepan, bring the water and salt to a boil. Clean the mushrooms, cutting a thin slice from the stem of each. Leave whole.
2. When the water is boiling, drop the mushrooms in for 2 minutes. Remove the mushrooms and place in a ceramic or stainless steel saucepan. Add ½ cup of the boiling water.

3. Add the vinegar, shallots, thyme, cayenne, and garlic, and simmer for 5 minutes. Remove from heat and stir in the oil, artichoke hearts and marinade, parsley, and pepper to taste.
4. Place the mixture in a glass or ceramic bowl, cover, and refrigerate for 24 hours. Toss gently a couple of times to coat the mushrooms with the marinade.

4 SERVINGS

Morels in Lemon Thyme Cream

A delicacy of the first order, morels are something mushroom hunters only whisper about. When they find a stand in the spring, they sneak them home, and even if they share the bounty with friends, they never share the location. They just hope the next spring will find morels growing there again. If you're not an expert but are keen for the hunt, take someone knowledgeable along. A mistake about mushrooms can be very serious.

> 1 pound fresh morels, cleaned and trimmed
> 2 tablespoons butter
> 1 tablespoon olive oil
> 1 tablespoon flour
> 1 teaspoon minced fresh lemon thyme
> 1 cup light cream
> 1 tablespoon Madeira wine
> 4 slices of fine-grained toasting bread

1. If the morels are very large, slice them in half. In a large skillet, sauté the morels in the butter and oil over medium-low heat for 10 minutes. They will be lightly browned.
2. Mix in the flour and lemon thyme and stir for about 2 minutes.
3. Add the cream and wine, cover, and simmer over very low heat for 10 minutes.

4. Toast the bread, cutting each slice into four triangles. Arrange the triangles on each plate like a pinwheel. When the mushrooms are cooked, serve immediately on the toast.

4 SERVINGS

Mushrooms Provençal

When a dish comes from Provence, it's filled with the aroma and taste of garlic, it contains the best of olive oils, and its basil is pungent and fresh. Think of rows of poplars, a green Mediterranean, and groves of olive trees while you stir these slices of porcini.

¾ pound porcini mushrooms
4 tablespoons extra virgin olive oil
2 tablespoons chopped fresh basil
2 garlic cloves, minced

Salt and freshly ground black pepper
Five thin slices of bread
¼ cup minced fresh parsley
1 teaspoon lemon juice

1. Clean the mushrooms and slice in pieces less than ¼-inch thick.
2. In a bowl, combine the mushroom slices with the oil, basil, garlic, and salt and pepper to taste. Toss gently to coat and set aside, unrefrigerated, for 30 minutes.
3. At serving time, sauté the mushroom mixture in a large skillet over medium-high heat, adding additional olive oil if it has all been absorbed.
4. Meanwhile, toast the bread. When the mushroom mixture is aromatic and nicely browned but not crisp, serve on the toast slices. Sprinkle the parsley and lemon juice over the top.

5 SERVINGS

Sautéed Shiitakes in Thyme

This recipe comes from Delftree Farm in North Adams, Massachusetts, where shiitakes are grown and distributed. Serve these mushrooms over toast points for a hearty first course or as a side dish with beef, pork, or duck. They may be cultivated, but they have a wild taste. Basil can be substituted for the thyme and rosemary.

1½ pounds shiitakes, caps only	½ teaspoon chopped fresh rosemary
4 tablespoons extra virgin olive oil	¼ cup dry white wine
2 garlic cloves, minced	½ cup tomato puree
2 tablespoons chopped fresh parsley	Salt and freshly ground black pepper
1 teaspoon fresh thyme leaves	

1. Thinly slice the mushrooms. Heat the oil in a large skillet and add the mushrooms, garlic, parsley, thyme, and rosemary. Partially cover the skillet and cook slowly over low heat, stirring from time to time, for about 10 minutes, or until the mushrooms have softened.
2. Stir in the wine and tomato puree. Simmer, uncovered, for another 10 minutes, or until the liquid in the pan has thickened. Season with salt and pepper to taste.

6 SERVINGS

Duxelles with Crostini

Duxelles is an elegant name for a simple garnish or stuffing concoction made of mushrooms. Once made, you can pop duxelles into a turkey, an omelette, or a sauce for chicken or fish. You can also use this herbed version as a spread for crostini — and try it with oregano or marjoram, too.

> 1 slim loaf of crusty Italian bread
> ¼ cup olive oil
> ½ pound crimini mushrooms, cleaned and trimmed
> 3 tablespoons butter
> 3 tablespoons minced scallions, white and an inch of green
> 2 tablespoons minced fresh tarragon
> 3 teaspoons minced fresh parsley
> Salt and freshly ground black pepper
> 2 tablespoons flour
> 3 tablespoons dry white wine

1. Cut the bread in ¼-inch slices. Brush with oil on both sides, and place on a nonstick cookie sheet, ready to bake and convert into crostini.
2. Mince the mushrooms. Melt the butter in a large skillet and let it foam. Add the minced scallions and cook, stirring, for about 3 minutes over medium heat.

3. Stir in the mushrooms, and continue to cook for another 3 to 4 minutes, until the mushrooms start to release liquid.
4. Preheat the oven to 400°F.
5. Stir the tarragon, parsley, salt and pepper to taste, flour, and white wine into the mushroom mixture. Lower the heat and cook until most of the moisture has evaporated. Remove from heat and let cool.
6. Bake the bread slices until they are crusty, about 10 minutes, turning them once. Serve with the duxelles.

¾ CUP

Porcini Country Pâté with Thyme and Sage

Country pâté need not be the high-fat version. You can make it with mushrooms and other vegetables and produce something interesting and nutritious. If you don't see kasha on the shelf, by the way, look for groats.

1 teaspoon butter
5 carrots
2 cups water
1 cup medium size kasha
4 cups packed whole spinach leaves
2 tablespoons safflower oil
2 cups thinly sliced porcini
   mushrooms
1 cup finely chopped scallions,
   green and white parts

¼ cup wheat germ
1 tablespoon spicy mustard
1 carton yolkless egg product or
   4 egg whites
2 teaspoons minced fresh sage
2 teaspoons minced fresh thyme
¼ cup minced fresh parsley
⅛ teaspoon hot chili oil
Salt and freshly ground black
   pepper

1. Lightly butter a 9 x 4-inch glass loaf pan.
2. Peel the carrots and shred three of them, leaving two whole. Cook the whole carrots in a little boiling water for about 15 minutes, or until tender.
3. In a saucepan, bring 2 cups of water to a boil, stir in the kasha, reduce the heat to low, and simmer for 10 minutes, or until the kasha is fluffy and the water absorbed. Leave covered.

4. Wash the spinach but do not drain. Put just enough water in a saucepan to cover the bottom, add the wet spinach, and steam over low heat for 4 to 5 minutes, or until wilted. Set aside.

5. Heat the safflower oil in a large skillet. Stir in the mushrooms, scallions, and shredded carrots, and cover and cook for about 5 minutes. When the mushrooms begin to release liquid, uncover the skillet, reduce the heat, and cook, stirring, until the vegetables are soft and the liquid is gone.

6. Remove the skillet from the stove, and preheat the oven to 350°F.

7. Stir the kasha until it is crumbly, and add it to the mushroom mixture. Stir in the wheat germ, mustard, egg product or egg whites, sage, thyme, parsley, chili oil, and salt and pepper to taste. Stir until well-blended.

8. Separate the spinach leaves, and line the loaf pan with them, overlapping the leaves and letting them hang over the top edge. Pack half of the mushroom mixture into the pan, put the two whole carrots in lengthwise, and pack in the rest of the mushroom mixture. Fold the spinach leaves over the top.

9. Cover the pâté with foil, making a few holes in the foil for steam vents. Put ½ inch of hot water in a roasting pan, and set the pâté pan in it. Bake for 1½ hours.

10. Cool the pâté on a rack for 30 minutes; then refrigerate for 24 hours. Turn the pâté onto a serving plate and use a sharp knife to slice it into ½-inch pieces.

16 SERVINGS

Savory Stuffed Caps

The classic white mushrooms found in every market are delicious when their stems are tweaked out, chopped up, and put back in the cap for baking. Their flavor blended with herbs and spicy sausage add a new twist to a favorite appetizer.

12 to 18 large white mushrooms
1 hot Italian sausage
½ cup fine bread crumbs
2 tablespoons red wine
2 garlic cloves

2 tablespoons chopped fresh parsley
1 tablespoon chopped fresh savory
2 tablespoons olive oil
2 tablespoons freshly grated
    Parmesan cheese

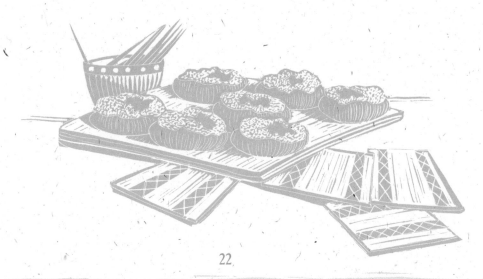

1. Clean the mushrooms. Remove the stems and chop finely.
2. Remove the casing from the Italian sausage, and crumble the meat into a small skillet over medium heat. Keep stirring with a fork to break up clumps, cooking the sausage until it is well-browned and crisp. Drain the meat on a paper towel.
3. Mix the chopped stems, bread crumbs, wine, garlic, parsley, savory, and 1 tablespoon of the oil. Add the mixture to the sausage and cook for a minute or two, stirring frequently. Mix in the cooked sausage.
4. Preheat the oven to 375°F. Brush the mushroom caps with the remaining oil and arrange them on a cookie sheet. Fill the caps with the sausage mixture, sprinkle with the Parmesan cheese, and bake until the mushrooms are golden, about 15 minutes.

1 TO 1½ DOZEN PIECES

Mushroom Bisque

Chopping wet herbs is a terrible business. They stick to your fingers, they stick to the cutting board, and they're tough to measure. So if you have to wash them at the last minute, put them in a paper towel and squeeze hard. And remember to remove the stems from thyme.

4 tablespoons unsalted butter
6 large shallots, finely chopped
1 garlic clove, minced
1 pound shiitakes, finely chopped
Juice of ½ lemon
1 tablespoon flour
3½ cups chicken or vegetable broth
1 teaspoon chopped fresh thyme

1 teaspoon chopped fresh tarragon
½ teaspoon salt
½ cup half-and-half
1 egg yolk
2 tablespoons Marsala wine
Salt and freshly ground black pepper
Low-fat sour cream (optional)

1. Melt 2 tablespoons of the butter in a large skillet over medium heat. Add the shallots and garlic and cook, stirring, for 5 minutes. Add the mushrooms and lemon juice and cook, stirring, for about 10 minutes. If the mushrooms begin to stick, add ¼ cup of the broth.
2. Melt the remaining 2 tablespoons of butter in a large saucepan over medium heat. Add the flour and cook, stirring for 5 minutes. Do not brown the flour. Gradually whisk in the broth, which should be at room temperature or slightly warmed.
3. When the mixture is smooth, add the mushroom mixture, thyme, tarragon, and salt. Reduce heat and simmer for 30 minutes.
4. Puree the soup in a food processor or blender and then strain through a fine sieve into a clean saucepan, rubbing the solids through with a wooden spoon.
5. Whisk the half-and-half and the egg yolk together in a bowl, and beat in about ½ cup of the hot soup. Add the mixture to the remaining soup and bring to a simmer, stirring. Do not boil.
6. Add the wine and season with salt and pepper to taste. Serve hot, adding a dollop of sour cream on top, if desired.

4–6 SERVINGS

Cream of Mushroom Soup
with Artichokes and Mint

This soup goes with a variety of finger foods — perhaps some chicken tenders, iced shrimp, carrot sticks, or whole green beans stir-fried with almonds — and cold beer. It's a combination of two exotic vegetables, enhanced by parsley and mint.

> 1 package (9-ounces) frozen artichoke hearts
> ½ cup chicken broth
> 3 tablespoons butter
> 4 shallots, finely chopped
> ½ pound fresh crimini mushrooms, cleaned and thinly sliced
> 2 tablespoons flour
> 1 tablespoon chopped fresh parsley
> 2 tablespoons chopped fresh mint
> 2 cups milk
> Salt and white pepper

1. Cook the artichoke hearts according to package directions and drain, reserving the cooking liquid. Stir the chicken broth into the artichoke liquid.

2. In a saucepan, sauté the shallots and mushrooms in the butter for about 10 minutes, or until the shallots are tender. Stir in the flour and parsley, and continue to cook over low heat until the mixture is bubbly and light brown.
3. Remove from heat and gradually stir in the broth, mint, and artichoke liquid. Add the milk. Reheat until the mixture thickens. Add salt and white pepper
   to taste.
4. Dice the artichoke hearts and add to the soup. Reheat to a simmer but do not allow to boil.

3–4 SERVINGS

Wild Mushroom Soup with Sage

You don't have to hunt wild mushrooms to get wild mushrooms. Supermarkets sell them. What they call "wild" mushrooms are actually pretty tame — they're grown on farms, just like most herbs.

¼ pound oyster mushrooms
¼ pound shiitakes
1½ pounds white button mushrooms
1 teaspoon extra virgin olive oil
1 small carrot, shredded
2 shallots, minced
1 garlic clove, peeled and chopped
2 teaspoons chopped fresh sage

1 scallion, green and white
   parts, chopped
2 teaspoons chopped fresh parsley
   plus 6 small sprigs for garnish
3 cups chicken broth
¼ teaspoon cayenne
Salt and freshly ground black pepper
2 tablespoons dry white wine

1. Clean and chop all the mushrooms, keeping the oyster and shiitake pieces separate from the button mushrooms. In a large saucepan, heat the oil over low heat. Add the oysters and shiitakes, carrot, shallots, garlic, sage, scallion, chopped parsley, and ½ cup of the chicken broth. Cook slowly until all the vegetables are soft, about ½ hour.
2. Add the remaining chicken broth, the button mushrooms, and the cayenne. Bring to a boil, then reduce heat and simmer until the mushrooms are soft, about 15 minutes.

3. Puree the soup in a food processor or blender, season with salt and pepper to taste, and return to the soup pot. Reheat until the soup is hot but not boiling.

4. Add the wine, transfer the soup to heated soup bowls, and garnish with a sprig of parsley.

6 SERVINGS

Clear Broth with Shiitake and Coriander

The hearty flavor of the shiitake (*shii* is the variety and *take* the Japanese word for mushroom), prized in Japan for centuries, combines with garlic and oregano in a clear, savory soup.

1½	teaspoons coriander seed
1½	teaspoons chopped fresh oregano
1½	teaspoons ground cumin
¼	teaspoon mustard seed
¼	teaspoon black peppercorns
1	pound shiitakes, coarsely chopped (about 15)
3	medium carrots, shredded
2	medium yellow onions, thinly sliced
5	scallions
2	ribs celery, thinly sliced
6	garlic cloves, lightly crushed
½	cup light soy sauce
2	quarts cold water
1	cup thinly sliced shiitake caps

1. Combine the coriander, oregano, cumin, mustard seed, and peppercorns in a small skillet. Stir constantly over medium heat, cooking until the spices and herbs are lightly toasted and aromatic.
2. Slice the whites of the scallions. Shred the green parts to make ½ cup and set aside.
3. In a large soup pot, combine the toasted flavorings with the chopped shiitakes, carrots, onions, sliced scallions, celery, garlic, soy sauce and water. Reduce the heat to medium-low and simmer gently for 1½ hours. The vegetables will be soft.
4. Pour the broth through a fine strainer or a colander lined with cheesecloth into a clean soup pot. Press the vegetables gently to extract as much liquid as possible.
5. Reheat the strained broth over medium heat. Add the sliced shiitake caps and simmer for 5 minutes, or until the caps are tender. Serve hot, sprinkled with the shredded scallion greens.

1 QUART

Shiitake Salad with Chervil

Raw mushrooms are soft, smooth, firm in texture, and hearty in flavor. They hint of the forest, of coolness, and of shade. In salads, especially with chervil, they are a welcome change from the usual vegetables.

 2 heads bibb lettuce
 ¼ cup extra virgin olive oil
 2 tablespoons sesame seeds
 Juice of ½ lemon (2 tablespoons)
 1 teaspoon sugar
 1 tablespoon light soy sauce
 ½ pound fresh shiitakes
 2 scallions, white and green parts, shredded
 3 teaspoons chopped fresh chervil

1. Separating the leaves, put the lettuce in a large bowl of cold water and wash by lifting the leaves out. Any sand will sift to the bottom, and the leaves will not get bruised. Place on paper towels to absorb as much moisture as possible.

2. In a small skillet, heat the oil and sesame seeds over low heat and cook for about 3 minutes, or until the seeds start to brown. Remove the pan from the heat and let cool. Stir in the lemon juice, sugar, and soy sauce. Set aside.

3. Rinse the mushrooms quickly and pat dry. Remove the stems and discard (or save them for soup). Slice the caps into ⅛-inch strips. Tear the lettuce and place in a salad bowl.
4. Add the mushrooms to the bowl, along with the scallions and the chervil. Pour in the sesame dressing, toss gently, and serve.

4 SERVINGS

Osaka Salad

The enoki mushroom is nothing short of exotic. Slender as a bean sprout but straighter, it's topped with the tiniest little beanie of a hat. Handle this delicate fungi with care.

3 cups of leaf lettuces (bibb, oak leaf, salad bowl, black-seeded Simpson)
1 cup fresh snow peas, with ends snipped off
2 tablespoons chopped fresh chervil
½ cup enoki mushrooms, with ends trimmed off
¼ teaspoon sugar
¼ cup rice wine vinegar
½ teaspoon soy sauce

1. Wash, drain, and chill the greens ahead of time. Steam the snow peas for no more than 5 minutes, cool under running water, drain, and chill.
2. Arrange the lettuce leaves and pea pods on individual salad plates and sprinkle with chervil. Top decoratively with the mushrooms.
3. Dissolve the sugar in the vinegar, stir in the soy sauce, and drizzle over the salad. Serve immediately.

4 SERVINGS

Hot Tarragon-Crimini Dressing

Try this dressing on a spinach salad, which will get just the right amount of wilt with the addition of the warm mixture. For a whole different flavor, substitute your favorite herbs for the tarragon and chives.

¼ cup extra virgin olive oil	¼ cup white wine vinegar
2 scallions, green and white parts	2 tablespoons minced fresh tarragon
8 ounces crimini mushrooms, cleaned and thinly sliced	1 tablespoon snipped fresh chives
	½ teaspoon honey
2 shallots, finely chopped	Salt and freshly ground black pepper

1. In a medium-sized nonstick ceramic or stainless steel skillet, warm the oil over medium heat.
2. Cut the scallions into 2-inch lengths, then shred lengthwise. Add the scallions, mushrooms, and shallots to the pan and cook for about 3 to 5 minutes, or until soft. Stir occasionally.
3. Add the vinegar, tarragon, chives, honey, and salt and pepper to taste, stirring to combine.
4. Serve immediately over a green salad that is mostly torn spinach leaves.

1 CUP

Grilled Shiitake with Potato Salad

The people at the Delftree mushroom farm in Western Massachusetts suggest wrapping fresh shiitakes in foil with a little butter and putting the package right on the grill. Add a little parsley and a teaspoon of capers to that package, and it will really sizzle. If you want to get a little fancier, try Delftree's grilled salad.

1 pound shiitakes, stems removed
12–17 tablespoons extra virgin
   olive oil
Juice of ½ lemon
Salt and freshly ground black pepper
2–3 potatoes
3 tablespoons white wine vinegar

1 garlic clove, finely chopped
2 shallots, finely chopped
1 teaspoon spicy mustard
2 tablespoons chopped fresh basil
2 tablespoons chopped fresh Italian
   flat-leaf parsley
2 large ripe tomatoes, cut into wedges

1. Clean the shiitakes and place in a large shallow dish. Toss with 2 tablespoons of the oil and sprinkle with the lemon juice. Season with salt and pepper to taste.
2. Scrub the potatoes, cut lengthwise into ½-inch slices, and place on a paper towel. Pat dry. Place the potatoes in another shallow dish and toss with 2 or 3 tablespoons of the olive oil. Season with salt and pepper to taste.
3. In a separate bowl, whisk together the vinegar, garlic, shallots, and mustard. Beat in 8 to 12 tablespoons of the oil and add the basil, parsley, and salt and pepper to taste.
4. With a slotted spatula, remove the mushrooms and potato slices from their dishes, letting the excess oil drip off. Grill the pieces over hot coals until tender and browned on both sides, brushing occasionally with the excess oil.
5. Arrange the grilled vegetables with the fresh tomato wedges on a serving plate, and spoon the dressing over the salad. Serve at room temperature.

4–6 SERVINGS

Stir-Fried Vegetables with Cilantro

When vegetables are plump with the moisture of freshness, they need little cooking. Combine them with fresh and dried mushrooms the Chinese way, and you'll discover that the chopping takes more time than the cooking. Tree ears — boxed — can be found with other Asian foods.

6 fresh shiitakes

6 dried tree ears, soaked in warm water for 20 minutes

20 fresh sugar pea pods

1 zucchini

3 tablespoons peanut oil

3 carrots, shredded

¼ pound fresh bean sprouts

½ cup chicken broth

½ cup dry white wine or rice wine

1 tablespoon cornstarch dissolved in 2 tablespoons water

3 scallions, green and white parts, shredded

3 tablespoons chopped fresh cilantro

1. Clean and slice the shiitakes, discarding the stems if they're tough. When the tree ears are done soaking, clip off the hard knobby part, rinse, pat dry, and chop.
2. Snip the strings off the pea pods. Finely chop the zucchini.
3. In a wok or large skillet, heat the oil. Stir-fry the zucchini for one minute. Add the mushrooms, tree ears, carrots, and bean sprouts, and keep tossing and stirring for 1 minute.
4. Add the broth and wine, along with the pea pods. Continue to scoop and turn the vegetables for 2 minutes over high heat. When the liquid boils, stir in the cornstarch, which has been dissolved in the water, and cook another 2 minutes or until the sauce starts to thicken.
5. Add the scallions and cilantro and mix quickly. Serve immediately.

4–5 SERVINGS

Crêpes with Herbed Wild Mushrooms

If crêpes cause you to panic a little, just think of them as pancakes on a diet. Sometimes they stick, and that's frustrating, but they're delicious and worth the trouble.

FOR THE CRÊPES

½ cup unbleached all-purpose flour	5 tablespoons butter
1 teaspoon baking powder	1 egg
Dash of salt	¾ cup milk, at room temperature

1. Sift together the flour, baking powder, and salt. Melt 2 tablespoons of the butter. Beat the egg until light, and slowly add the milk and melted butter. Gradually add the egg mixture to the sifted dry ingredients and beat until smooth and bubbly, using an electric mixer or whisk.

2. Heat a crêpe-sized skillet (6 inches) and add ¼ teaspoon of the butter. Pour 2 tablespoonfuls of batter quickly into the skillet, and then quickly tilt the pan so the mixture spreads evenly over the bottom. When the crêpe is brown on one side, turn it and brown the other side.

3. Repeat, adding another ¼ teaspoon of butter for each crêpe.

FOR THE FILLING

¼ pound crimini mushrooms

½ pound shiitakes

¼ cup butter

2 teaspoons minced fresh thyme

2 teaspoons minced fresh rosemary

½ teaspoon light soy sauce

Juice of ½ lemon

Salt and freshly ground black pepper

1. Clean and chop the mushrooms. In a medium skillet, melt the butter and cook the mushrooms for 2 minutes, tossing gently.
2. As they start to become golden, add the thyme, rosemary, soy sauce, lemon juice, and salt and pepper to taste. Remove from heat while making the sauce.

FOR THE SAUCE

3 tablespoons butter

3 tablespoons unbleached all-purpose flour

3 cups chicken broth

1 garlic clove on a toothpick

½ cup light cream

¼ cup Marsala wine

1. In a saucepan, brown the butter and flour, stirring them together. Stir in the broth and whisk to remove all lumps. Add the garlic clove and, over low heat, cook covered for 20 minutes, stirring occasionally. When the liquid is reduced to about 2 cups, add the light cream and wine.
2. Preheat the broiler. Remove the garlic clove. Divide the filling among the crêpes and roll them up. With the edge side down, place the crêpes on a lightly greased, broilerproof pan. Pour the sauce over the top and broil for 2 minutes or less.

6 SERVINGS (12 CRÊPES)

Risotto with Mushrooms

In Italy, risotto is both classic and commonplace. In America, it's made only where cooks are patient and willing to stir. And stir. And stir. But it's worth it. You'll need to look for Arborio rice if you're going to do it right.

5½ cups chicken broth

4 ounces crimini mushrooms, cleaned and sliced

1 medium leek, white part only, halved lengthwise and carefully washed and chopped

1 cup fresh or frozen green peas

2 tablespoons butter

2 tablespoons extra virgin olive oil

2 tablespoons minced yellow onion

2 cups Arborio rice, dark grains removed

½ cup dry white wine

½ cup chopped fresh Italian flat-leaf parsley

1 ounce Fontina cheese, diced (¼ cup)

Salt and freshly ground black pepper

1. In a saucepan, bring the broth to a boil over medium heat. Add the mushrooms, leek, and peas; turn the heat to low and simmer for 3 minutes, or until the vegetables are almost tender. Lift the vegetables from the broth with a strainer and transfer them to a bowl. Keep the broth simmering.

2. In a large, heavy saucepan, heat the butter and oil and cook the minced onion slowly until almost translucent. Do not brown it. Add the rice, stirring quickly to coat the grains with oil and butter.

3. Add the wine and cook, stirring constantly, until all the liquid has been absorbed. Make sure the rice does not stick to the pan. Add 1½ cups of the simmering broth, continuing to stir, and cook the rice until the liquid is gone. Keep adding broth, a cup at a time, stirring and cooking after each addition until the liquid is gone. When 4½ cups of broth have been added, the rice will start to be tender.

4. Stir in the mushrooms, leek, and peas, along with the last cup of broth. Simmer for another 3 to 4 minutes, or until the liquid has been absorbed, making a total of 30 to 35 minutes of cooking time for the rice. If the rice is not tender, add a little more broth and cook a few extra minutes.

5. Stir in the parsley, cheese, and salt and pepper to taste, and serve.

6 SERVINGS

Herbed Veggie Pie

When this pie is opened, even the nonvegetarians begin to sing because, indeed, it is a dainty dish to set before the king — or any of his herb-loving subjects.

FOR THE PASTRY
1⅓ cups unbleached all-purpose flour
1 stick butter, very cold
¼ cup ice water

FOR THE PIE FILLING
1 cup carrots, cut on a slant in thin slices
1 cup broccoli florets, separated
1 cup fresh or frozen pea pods, sliced in half
½ pound crimini or other wild mushrooms, sliced
1 onion, coarsely chopped
3 tablespoons extra virgin olive oil

3 tablespoons cornstarch
¼ cup chopped fresh parsley
1 tablespoon chopped fresh sage
Salt and freshly ground black pepper
1 cup vegetable cooking water
1 cup milk, at room temperature
1 teaspoon butter
¼ pound bean sprouts, chopped

1. Preheat the oven to 400°F. Cut the butter into 1-inch pieces and put into the bowl of a food processor with the flour. Process for about 8 seconds. With the processor still running, pour in the ice water, mixing until the dough forms into a ball. Remove the ball of pastry, cover tightly with plastic wrap, and refrigerate.

2. Cook the carrots, broccoli, and pea pods separately until they are just tender, not mushy. Combine the cooking liquid from each and reserve. In a large bowl, combine the vegetables with the mushrooms.
3. In a small saucepan, cook the onion gently in the oil until golden but not crisp. Stir in the cornstarch, parsley, sage, and salt and pepper to taste, and whisk until smooth. Add the cup of vegetable cooking water and the milk and cook until the sauce has the smooth consistency of white sauce. If it's too thick, add more vegetable liquid or milk.
4. Add the sauce to the vegetables and toss gently to combine. Butter a 3-quart casserole and add the bean sprouts.
5. On a lightly floured board, roll out the pastry, fit it over the top of the casserole, crimp the edges to seal, and prick the top with a fork to allow steam to escape. Bake for 30 minutes, or until the pastry is golden and the sauce is bubbling through the vents. Serve immediately with a large green salad.

6 SERVINGS

Mushrooms, Sun-Dried Tomatoes, and Pasta

If you can find angel-hair pasta with spinach or red pepper flavoring, it's worth a try with this dish. Otherwise, plain fresh pasta will do nicely. Remember not to overcook fresh pasta — it's out of the water almost as soon as it goes in.

½ cup butter
6 garlic cloves, chopped
¾ pound wild mushrooms, shiitake or crimini, coarsely chopped
2 tablespoons chopped fresh basil
3 tablespoons chopped fresh parsley
¼ cup oil-packed, sun-dried tomatoes, chopped
2 cups half-and-half
Salt and white pepper
1 package (16 ounces) fresh angel hair or other fresh pasta

1. Fill a large pot with water for the pasta and heat to boiling.
2. While the water heats, melt the butter in a large skillet and sauté the garlic for 2 minutes. Add the mushrooms and cook over low heat for another 3 minutes.

3. Stir in the basil, parsley, and sun-dried tomatoes, then gradually pour in the half-and-half, stirring constantly. Simmer slowly for 5 to 7 minutes, or until the half-and-half is reduced and the sauce thickens. Add salt and white pepper to taste.
4. Cook the pasta according to the package directions. Drain and serve immediately, topped with the sauce.

6 SERVINGS

Herbed Mushrooms
and Tomatoes in Sherry

For a quick supper, try mushrooms with tomatoes over rice. A bit of basil, some parsley, and black olives add elegance to a simple dish. To peel the tomato easily, drop it in boiling water for 15 seconds, then rinse it in cold water.

2 cups long-grain white rice
5 tablespoons butter
1 pound fresh crimini mushrooms,
   sliced
1 tomato, peeled and chopped
1 garlic clove, minced

1 tablespoon chopped fresh basil
½ cup sherry
Salt and freshly ground black pepper
4 tablespoons chopped fresh parsley
12 black olives, chopped

1. Cook the rice according to the package instructions.
2. Ten minutes before the rice is done, melt the butter in a large skillet. Sauté the mushrooms, tomato, garlic, and basil for 5 minutes. Stir in the sherry and salt and pepper to taste.
3. Cook another 5 minutes, stirring constantly. Place the cooked rice in a pasta-style bowl, pour the mushroom and tomato mixture on top, and sprinkle with the parsley and chopped olives.

4 SERVINGS

Portabella and Basil Sauce for Pasta

Buy a package of fresh linguine, which needs only a minute or two of cooking, and serve it with this light, chunky sauce that combines the flavors of fresh portabella mushrooms, ripe tomatoes, and basil.

¾ pound portabella mushrooms
2 tablespoons extra virgin olive oil
2 garlic cloves, put through a press
1 can (6 ounces) tomato paste
8 medium fully ripe tomatoes, chopped

¼ cup chopped fresh basil
2 tablespoons chopped fresh parsley
Salt and freshly ground black pepper
¼ cup freshly grated Parmesan cheese
¼ cup freshly grated Romano cheese

1. Slice the mushrooms, then cut the slices in half. (You should have about 2 cups.) In a large skillet, gently cook the mushrooms in the oil for 7 to 8 minutes. Add the garlic and cook another 3 to 4 minutes.
2. Stir in the tomato paste and the chopped tomatoes. Season with the basil, parsley, and salt and pepper to taste, and cook over medium heat for 1 hour.
3. Combine the two cheeses and add to the sauce. Cook another five minutes to melt the cheese. Serve over hot pasta.

6 SERVINGS

Savory Mushroom Sauce

For scrod, halibut, or rice, this mushroom sauce — made with either white button mushrooms or the more flavorful porcini — is overflowing with fresh herbs. The chervil (reputedly a cure for poor memory) doesn't stand for much cooking, so it goes in last.

2 tablespoons extra virgin olive oil
1 Spanish or Vidalia onion,
   thinly sliced
1 cup sliced button or porcini
   mushrooms
½ cup dry white wine

½ cup chicken broth
2 teaspoons chopped fresh thyme
1 teaspoon chopped fresh savory
Salt and freshly ground black pepper
2 teaspoons chopped fresh chervil

1. Heat the oil in a medium-sized skillet and cook the onion over low heat for 10 minutes, taking care not to let the slices brown. When they are golden, add the mushrooms and cook for another 5 minutes, tossing gently.
2. Add the wine and broth and simmer until the liquid is reduced. Add the thyme, savory, and salt and pepper to taste, and simmer for another 5 minutes. Stir in the chervil, cook 1 minute, and remove the pan from the heat. The sauce can be refrigerated for a number of hours and reheated just before serving.

ABOUT 1¼ CUPS

Citrus Salsa with Mushrooms

You can try this salsa with chips if you like, but it's recommended as a sauce for grilled swordfish, a substitute for mayonnaise in a sliced chicken sandwich, or a side dish with roast tenderloin of pork. For a change of pace, try half a mango in place of the orange.

1 large (4- to 5-inch diameter) portabella mushroom
1 orange, peeled, seeded, and diced
½ cucumber, finely chopped
1 Granny Smith apple, unpeeled, diced
8 Greek olives, pitted and chopped
1 jalapeño pepper, cored, seeded, and minced
1 tablespoon minced fresh mint
1 teaspoon minced fresh cilantro
1 tablespoon minced fresh parsley
Juice of 1 lime

1. Remove and discard the mushroom stem (or save it for soup), clean the cap, and chop the mushroom.
2. In a medium-sized bowl, gently toss the mushroom with the orange, cucumber, apple, olives, pepper, mint, cilantro, parsley, and lime juice.
3. Let stand at room temperature for at least 1 hour before serving.

1½–2 CUPS

Mushrooms with Parsleyed Sole

Standard white mushrooms, long a staple of produce departments, work just fine with this recipe, but for a little extra flavor, try crimini — their shape is similar, but their caps are nut brown, and their taste is heartier. As for the parsley, Italian flat leaf has a stronger taste than its curly-headed cousin, which will add zest to both the mushrooms and the sweet sole.

1 tablespoon plus 1 teaspoon butter
1½ pounds sole fillets
2 tablespoons extra virgin olive oil
1 sweet onion, finely chopped
¼ cup chopped fresh Italian parsley
2 tablespoons chopped fresh dill
2 teaspoons minced fresh tarragon
1 tablespoon snipped fresh chives
½ pound white or crimini mushrooms
½ teaspoon freshly ground black pepper
¼ cup white wine
1 tablespoon flour
½ cup low-fat milk
⅛ teaspoon cayenne

1. Preheat oven to 350°F. Using a teaspoon of the butter, lightly coat a casserole dish. Rinse fish in salted water, then in plain water. Pat dry.
2. Heat the oil in a medium skillet and sauté the onion for 2 minutes; then add the parsley, dill, tarragon, chives, and mushrooms, and continue cooking over low heat until the onion is soft. Stir frequently.
3. Place half of the sole in the casserole and sprinkle with half of the pepper. Spread the onion and mushroom mixture over the fish, topping it with the remaining fillets and the rest of the pepper. Pour the wine over the top and dot with the rest of the butter.
4. Bake for 15 minutes, uncovered. Remove from the oven, and drain off the liquid, reserving it. In a saucepan over low heat, whisk together the flour, milk, and cayenne. Add the reserved liquid and cook, stirring, until it thickens.
5. Pour the sauce over the fish and bake for another 5 to 7 minutes.

4–5 SERVINGS

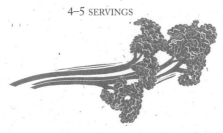

Mushroom Tart with Dilly Scallops

You can use the flowers and the leaves of dill in this dish. Today, dill grows wild and will seed itself in the garden, but in Biblical times in what is now the Middle East, it was so valuable as medicine that it was subject to a tithe.

6 tablespoons butter
3 tablespoons flour
1½ cups milk, at room temperature
⅛ teaspoon cayenne
¼ teaspoon white pepper
2 tablespoons finely snipped dill
Salt
1 pound bay scallops (if large ones
    are used, dice them)
¼ cup dry white wine

1 pound crimini mushrooms
1 egg yolk
2 tablespoons light cream or
    half-and-half
2 tablespoons sherry
6 tart shells (see pastry recipe on
    page 44)
1 flower head of dill or 6 parsley
    sprigs for garnish

1. Melt 3 tablespoons of the butter in a large saucepan. Stir in the flour, gradually stir in the milk, and cook over low heat, stirring constantly, until thickened. Add the cayenne, white pepper, dill, and salt to taste.
2. Place the scallops in a shallow pan, add water almost to cover, and then add the wine. Bring to a boil, reduce heat immediately, and poach gently for 5 minutes. Drain.

3. Add the scallops to the white sauce. Sauté the mushrooms in a skillet in the remaining 3 tablespoons of butter, and add to the white sauce.

4. Just before serving, stir in the egg yolk, cream or half-and-half, and sherry, and heat almost to the boiling point. Spoon into the tart shells. Divide the dill head by florets, and garnish each tart. Parsley can be substituted as a garnish.

6 SERVINGS

Rosemary Chicken with Crimini and Roasted Peppers

Along with taste, appearance matters in cooking. This dish, redolent of rosemary and garnished with a couple of curly parsley sprigs, creates a splash on a plate.

1 large red bell pepper
2 chicken breasts, halved, skinned, and boned
4 tablespoons flour
Freshly ground black pepper
2 tablespoons extra virgin olive oil
2 tablespoons butter
½ cup dry white wine
1 tablespoon chopped fresh rosemary
2 scallions, green and white parts, shredded
½ pound crimini mushrooms, cleaned and sliced
¼ cup chopped fresh parsley

1. Heat the broiler. Slice the pepper in half lengthwise, remove the seeds, and place skin side up on a broiling pan. Broil for 5 minutes, or until the skin chars. Remove the pepper halves from the oven, pop them into a plastic bag, and close the bag tightly. Leave for 10 minutes.
2. Cut each half breast of chicken into three pieces. Place flour and black pepper for seasoning in a plastic bag, and toss the chicken in the peppered flour. Heat the oil and butter in a large skillet, shake the excess flour off each chicken piece, and brown the chicken on all sides. Turn the heat down and continue to cook for 5 minutes. Remove the chicken to a plate.
3. Add the wine to the skillet and, over low heat, add the rosemary, scallions, and mushrooms. Cook gently for 5 minutes, stirring frequently and loosening any chicken fragments that are stuck to the pan.
4. In the meantime, remove the pepper halves from the bag and peel. Cut them into lengthwise strips and add to the skillet.
5. Return the chicken pieces to the skillet, stirring to combine all ingredients. Continue to cook and stir until the chicken is thoroughly cooked, adding more wine if necessary. Stir in the parsley, cook 1 minute, and serve.

4–5 SERVINGS

Turkey with Wild Mushrooms and Tarragon

People's noses tend to turn up when anyone says "leftovers." But leftover turkey is an exception. Here, ensconced in the woodsiness of wild mushrooms and the fresh taste of tarragon, it maintains its reputation as a leftover worth eating. If you have a microwave oven, make the white sauce there. As for the mushrooms, sometimes they come in a mixed pack, which is what was used here. Otherwise, pick your own mix or use one variety.

1 pound fresh asparagus
2 tablespoons butter
3 tablespoons unbleached all-purpose flour
1½ cups chicken broth
½ teaspoon salt
½ pound wild mushrooms (crimini, oyster, shiitake), chopped
2 cups diced cooked turkey
2 tablespoons minced fresh parsley
2 teaspoons minced fresh tarragon
White pepper

1. Wash the asparagus spears, break off the tough ends, and cut into 2-inch pieces holding the knife at a slant. Steam for 5 minutes in a small amount of water. Drain and set aside.

2. In a microwave-safe bowl, melt the butter. Stir in the flour until the mixture is smooth, and then slowly stir in the chicken broth. Return to the microwave for 4 to 5 minutes, stirring after each minute of cooking. The white sauce should thicken.
3. Add the salt and wild mushrooms to the sauce.
4. Preheat the oven to 375°F and grease a shallow 2-quart casserole.
5. Place the asparagus in the casserole, cover with the diced turkey, and sprinkle the parsley and tarragon over the top. Add white pepper to taste.
6. Pour the mushroom sauce mixture over the top and bake uncovered for 25 minutes.

6 SERVINGS

Veal Scallopini with Sage

Shop for pale pink or white scallops of veal and fresh wild mushrooms, and you have the makings of a feast. Sage, usually reserved for the Thanksgiving turkey, goes well with the woodsy taste of the mushrooms. Serve with linguine tossed in garlicky olive oil and a salad of fresh greens, thinly sliced cucumbers, parsley, and diced oranges.

3 tablespoons unbleached flour
Freshly ground black pepper
¾ pound veal scallopini, pounded thin
2 tablespoons extra virgin olive oil
4 shallots, chopped
¼ pound shiitake or crimini mushrooms, sliced
2 tablespoons butter
2 teaspoons chopped fresh sage
¼ cup chopped fresh parsley
Juice of 1 lemon
½ cup dry white wine

1. Mix the flour with pepper to taste. Dredge the veal in the seasoned flour.
2. In a large heavy skillet, heat the oil until quite hot and quickly brown the veal scallops, cooking them for 1 or 2 minutes on each side. Remove them to a plate.
3. Add the shallots to the pan and cook them for about 1 minute, stirring constantly. Add in the sliced mushrooms, cooking them for 2 minutes.
4. Add the butter, and when it's melted, return the veal and any juice from the plate to the pan, turning the slices to coat them with butter. Add the sage, parsley, lemon juice, and wine; cook until the veal scallops are hot and the sauce is brown and thickened.

4 SERVINGS

Index

Converting Recipe Measurements to Metric

Use the following formulas for converting U.S. measurements to metric. Since the conversions are not exact, it's important to convert the measurements for all of the ingredients to maintain the same proportions as the original recipe.

WHEN THE MEASUREMENT GIVEN IS	MULTIPLY IT BY	TO CONVERT TO
teaspoons	4.93	milliliters
tablespoons	14.79	milliliters
fluid ounces	29.57	milliliters
cups (liquid)	236.59	milliliters
cups (liquid)	.236	liters
cups (dry)	275.31	milliliters
cups (dry)	.275	liters
pints (liquid)	473.18	milliliters
pints (liquid)	.473	liters
pints (dry)	550.61	milliliters
pints (dry)	.551	liters
quarts (liquid)	946.36	milliliters
quarts (liquid)	.946	liters
quarts (dry)	1101.22	milliliters
quarts (dry)	1.101	liters
gallons	3.785	liters
ounces	28.35	grams
pounds	.454	kilograms
inches	2.54	centimeters
degrees Fahrenheit	$\frac{5}{9}$ (temperature − 32)	degrees Celsius

While standard metric measurements for dry ingredients are given as units of mass, U.S. measurements are given as units of volume. Therefore, the conversions listed above for dry ingredients are given in the metric equivalent of volume.